THE ESSENTIAL GUIDE

Written by Glenn Dakin

Contents

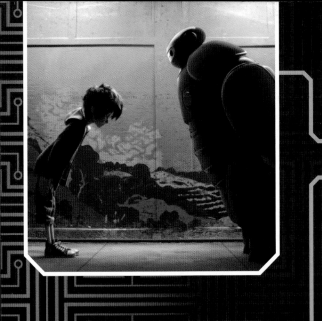

Introduction

Welcome to San Fransokyo! In this gadget-crazy city there's one boy whose offbeat genius towers above the rest—it's just that nobody has noticed it yet. Hiro Hamada is a 14-year-old robotics whiz who could change the world... if he ever stops fooling around.

It's lucky Hiro has some of the coolest super-nerd friends in the world. Honey, Wasabi, and Go Go are all bright sparks at San Fransokyo Institute of Technology, the school Hiro dreams of going to. And then there's Fred. The less said about him the better.

One day, all Hiro's dreams of greatness may come true. But first he's going to face a massive challenge, a sinister foe, and a mystery that takes him far beyond the streets he loves so much. Oh, and he's going to end up friends with a giant robot along the way. Step into Hiro's world and let the big hero action begin!

San Fransokyo

Glittering skyscrapers soar above the crowded streets and shadowy back alleys of this city that combines old and new in endless exciting ways. In San Fransokyo, science and technology are everywhere, and anyone with creativity and determination can rise up to become a hero.

Neon signs are in multiple languages

24-hour animated billboards

Where East meets West

Asian-influenced architecture and ramshackle noodle-bars sit side by side with hot dog stands and stately skyscrapers. The unique fusion flavor of this metropolis makes it an exciting place to be.

DID YOU KNOW?

San Fransokyo is built to withstand earthquakes, and its buildings are designed to survive swaying and shaking.

City of invention

Animated neon signs dazzle the eyes, colorful vending machines squeeze into every corner, and wind turbines fill the air like hovering zeppelins. San Fransokyo is a city of invention, where crime lords are more likely to have a bot fight than a gang war.

Aerial turbines produce power from the wind

Skybridges connect soaring towers

Jewel of the Pacific

A thriving city by the bay, San Fransokyo is a glittering jewel on the Pacific Rim. A multicultural metropolis, it is an example of a world where East meets West. Art and technology blend beautifully in this prosperous city.

Mass transit cable car system

Hiro

Meet Hiro Hamada! He may just be the brainiest kid in San Fransokyo, although don't tell him that. Inventive Hiro is crazy about building robots and is an expert in battle bots. Someday his genius could help the world—if he ever decides to break free of the battle bot fighting circuit.

Big brother knows best

Hiro's big brother Tadashi has always been there for him. He encourages Hiro's ideas—no matter how crazy—and tries to keep him out of trouble!

Nimble fingers for fine tech-work

Battle bot king

Two bots enter—one bot leaves! Hiro knows all there is to know about street bot fighting. When he takes on Mr. Yama, the local champ, the battle lasts only seconds... and Hiro is the winner!

"IF I DON'T GO TO THIS NERD SCHOOL, I'M GOING TO LOSE MY MIND."

Cool hair should never look combed

T-shirt reveals love of armored warrior bots

Comfortable and cool hoodie to wear at bot fights

Hiro's hideaway

In addition to his garage workshop, this bedroom is where Hiro has some of his best ideas. The shelves show how his love of robot toys evolved into him building his own creations.

Nerd heaven

Hiro thinks college is just a place where they tell you stuff you already know—until Tadashi takes him to his lab at San Fransokyo Tech. There Hiro meets his own hero, Professor Callaghan, author of "Callaghan's Law of Robotics." Suddenly college is the one place Hiro wants to be.

DID YOU KNOW?

Hiro's battle robot, "Megabot," has an edge— it is held together magnetically, so it can reassemble itself!

11

Tadashi

Kind, thoughtful, and always dependable, Tadashi is the best big brother Hiro can imagine. He always gives Hiro sensible advice, and whenever Hiro doesn't take it—which is most days—big bro is still there to get him out of trouble.

DID YOU KNOW?

Tadashi has sown mini GPS systems into every one of Hiro's hoodies, so he can keep tabs on his little brother.

Three's company

Three is the magic number for Tadashi's close-knit family unit. Aunt Cass looks after her nephews and they bring fun into her life.

School of hard knocks

Despite their caring relationship, the boys still love to fight and score points off each other. Martial arts bouts remind Hiro that Tadashi is still the boss!

Favorite
baseball cap

Fearless friend

Tadashi's super-
sensible exterior
hides a brave heart.
He will always help
out anyone in danger,
no matter what the
cost to himself.

Stylish yet
casual jacket

"I'M NOT GIVING UP ON YOU."

Changing the world

Don't let that relaxed look
fool you—Tadashi is a tough,
determined character who works
all hours to perfect his "Baymax"
personal healthcare companion.
He feels passionately that
science should free people
from suffering and all his
energy is invested in his
project. More than anything,
Tadashi wants Baymax to
help a lot of people.

Man-bag for
gadgets and
research notes

Aunt Cass

Family comes first for Hiro's aunt, who has raised him and his brother ever since they were small. From her beloved café she keeps an eye on their comings and goings, and is sure to keep her customers up to speed with all their achievements.

The Lucky Cat Café

A hardworking, talented chef, Cass has built up a great little reputation for her café. Cass is business-savvy, too—she organizes special events to drum up new customers.

DID YOU KNOW?

Cass has a soft spot for poetry, and often runs evening poetry readings at the café.

Meet Mochi

Cass's cat, Mochi, loves the attention he gets from the café customers. Things can go a little too far though, when Hiro and Tadashi invent new things for Mochi to try out!

Wild hair is Cass's trademark

"I LOVE MY FAMILY."

Turquoise gemstone symbolizes wisdom

Black t-shirt hides coffee stains

Aunt in a million

The one thing that makes Cass burst with pride are the achievements of her boys. Her big dream is to see them studying at college together.

Secret of success

Aunt Cass provides Hiro and Tadashi with garage space to turn into a lab, feeds them brain-nurturing food, and listens to their problems. She keeps everyone together, and is the boys' biggest supporter.

15

Miniature Japanese lanterns

Antique Italian coffee grinder

Cherry blossom sprig for extra good luck

Tea-lights keep teapots warm

The Lucky Cat Café

Aunt Cass's café is her pride and joy and is a cool, cozy hangout for young and old. It is named after the traditional lucky cat ornament—or "beckoning cat" as it is sometimes called—with its right paw raised to bring good fortune.

Home-from-home

The café is like a second home for Hiro and his friends, who can always drop in for a warm welcome or even a shoulder to cry on. It also has many other regulars, like Mrs. Matsuda, an 80-year-old who likes to wear age-inappropriate clothing.

Door to apartment upstairs

Table for two, for friendly chats

Aunt Cass's menu

Hiro's aunt mixes a healthy approach—selling smoothies and fruit teas—with a love of treats. One of her specials is *Yakisoba-pan*, a chow mein hot dog.

San Fransokyo Tech

Every science student in the city dreams of winning a place at San Fransokyo Institute of Technology (SFIT). While its futuristic architecture catches the eye, the rest of the campus was actually created over 100 years ago. Beautiful landscaped gardens contain peaceful lakes with traditional Japanese-style footbridges.

Round windows enhance flowing design

Flower gardens create tranquil environment

Professor Callaghan

Robotics Professor Robert Callaghan is a legend at SFIT, and famous around the world as the inventor of "Callaghan's Law of Robotics." He demands 100% commitment from his students, and says they are there to shape the future.

Solar panels
in roof

Smart
windows filter
sunlight

Cherry blossom
trees decorate
the grounds

ITO ISHIOKA
ROBOTICS LAB

Lab named
after Professor
Ito Ishioka

Robotics Lab

This cutting-edge building is as innovative as the projects inside it. Its three floors are divided into futuristic labs that offer privacy when needed, alongside fun places to swap ideas. The glass exterior lets in natural light, while solar panels provide the energy it needs.

Baymax

Baymax is a personal healthcare companion. He can scan any human, diagnose a problem, and provide treatment. His creator, Tadashi, knows that pain isn't just physical, so Baymax can download solutions to other problems, too. His inflatable form makes him very huggable.

DID YOU KNOW?

Baymax needs regular recharging, or he begins to deflate, muddles his words, and becomes very slow.

Persistent carer

Baymax is programmed with more than 10,000 different medical procedures, representing a serious piece of computer coding by Tadashi. He is activated by any cry of human pain and will not stop helping his patient until they state that they are satisfied with their care.

"HELLO. I AM BAYMAX, YOUR PERSONAL HEALTHCARE COMPANION."

Soft but strong

Under his cuddly exterior, Baymax has a carbon fiber skeleton that is close to unbreakable. Powerful motors and inflatable inner sections give him enormous strength.

Cute face to
calm patients

Access port for
chip insertion

Nurse chip

A nurse chip built
by Tadashi controls
Baymax's functions
and governs his
behavior. With his
nurse chip in, he will
never harm a human.

Travel mode

Baymax is designed to be
easily transportable. His
skeleton folds away, so
that when he deflates
he fits snugly into his
wheeled traveling case.

Inflatable
vinyl skin

21

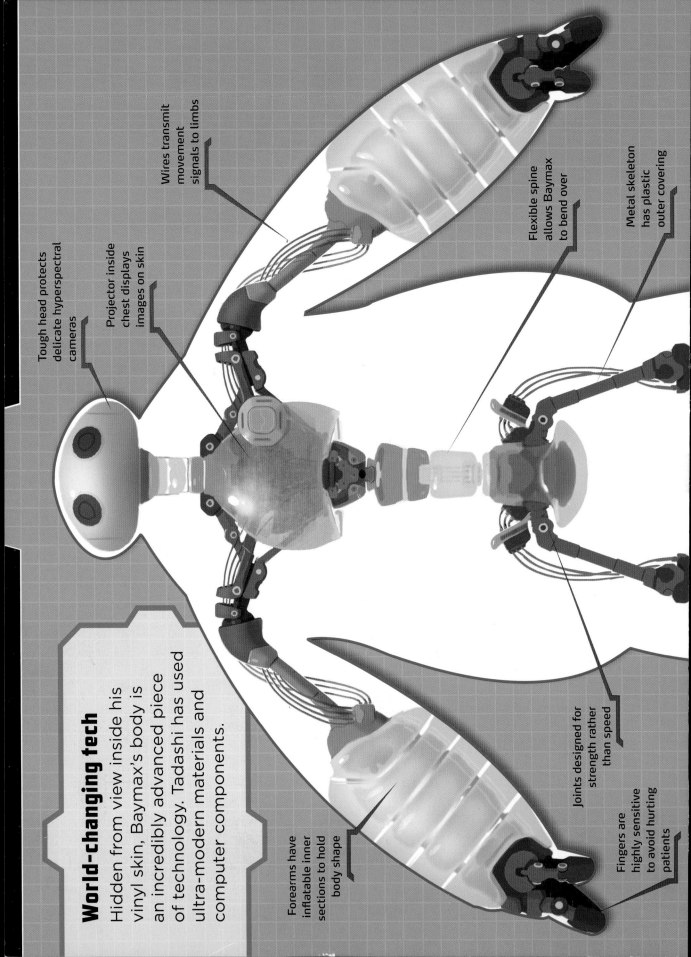

World-changing tech

Hidden from view inside his vinyl skin, Baymax's body is an incredibly advanced piece of technology. Tadashi has used ultra-modern materials and computer components.

Tough head protects delicate hyperspectral cameras

Projector inside chest displays images on skin

Wires transmit movement signals to limbs

Flexible spine allows Baymax to bend over

Metal skeleton has plastic outer covering

Forearms have inflatable inner sections to hold body shape

Joints designed for strength rather than speed

Fingers are highly sensitive to avoid hurting patients

Baymax's Body

At first glance, Baymax might not look like an amazing piece of futuristic design—but it is what's on the inside that counts. His true strength lies in his strong, flexible skeleton and his revolutionary computer brain. Healthcare will never be the same again!

Limbs retract when Baymax enters travel/storage mode

Emergency repairs
Baymax is programmed to repair himself in the event of damage. When his outer skin is punctured, Baymax uses tape to plug the holes!

A tight spot
Being soft and huggable is useful for a personal healthcare companion, but not always practical. Baymax can deflate and then reinflate to squeeze through small spaces.

Go Go

Go Go combines a brilliant engineering mind with an insane love of extreme velocity. She likes building cutting-edge bikes with electro-magnetic suspension—then she usually recycles the wheels to make something even speedier!

Purple streak in hair shows punky attitude

Tadashi's team

Despite her tough, independent streak, Go Go is an integral member of Tadashi's team. She provides the cool attitude and the bold one-liners.

Tight clothes for less air resistance in motion

The quiet type

She may not be the chattiest character around, but when Go Go **does** speak, people listen. She has strong opinions about most things, which can annoy people, but her friends trust her instincts.

Wasabi

This super-organized nerd is a physics genius, but behind his swagger he is really very cautious and a neat-freak. However, he supports his pals to the max, even providing fresh underpants and breath mints at crucial moments.

Everything in its place

Wasabi goes to incredible lengths to keep his work area pristine and in perfect order. There are even outlines on his desk to show exactly where each tool should go!

Big man on campus

Wasabi is a well-known figure at SFIT, with his powerful physique and big personality. His laser systems are so amazing that some students think he can invent anything—his friend Fred has asked for a laser to shrink himself with.

Honey

Honey is an eternal optimist who can see the bright side of everything—even when faced with terrible situations. Hiro thinks she is the happiest person on Earth, and whenever he is down she is quick to understand his sadness and give him support.

Glasses double as lab safety goggles

Posing for a photo

Chemistry whiz

Honey is a chemistry genius, and is able to create all kinds of amazing mixtures. She has even invented a special pink goo that can turn the toughest metals into dust.

Stylish cardigan shows her keen fashion sense

Positive power

Honey's sunny personality means she loves life and can see the magic in every minute. She enjoys taking selfies, encouraging her friends, and getting really excited about stuff. She also has a tough side—and an unexpected love of extreme danger.

Fred

Fred is no science geek—
he just likes hanging out
with people who are. More
than anything, he dreams
of becoming a super hero.
And just like a super hero,
he lives a secret double life...

One of Fred's
collection of
beanies

Limited edition
Kentucky Kaiju
pendant

KENTUCKY KAIJU

大乱闘 ケンタッキー怪獣

AWAKENING JULY 11

ついに、アイツがやって来る―。

怪獣

AN UNDERGROUND SMASH

Z FILM

A FELIX • GIAMPA • BRADLEY PRODUCTION
IN ASSOCIATION WITH CAITLIN FILMS

The super-nerd

An expert on super
heroes, Fred
knows the plot of
every comic ever
written and expects
real life to be just
like them. He even
collects original
movie monster suits.

T-shirt once
owned by
creator of
Megazon comic

Weird but wealthy

Fred may look like he sleeps
under a bridge, but his friends
don't realize he actually comes
from a mega-rich family.
He even has a butler named
Heathcliff, and his parents
"vacay" on their own island.

The Tech Showcase

Every year, San Fransokyo Tech prepares for a new influx of students with its traditional battle of the brains—the SFIT Tech Showcase. The event attracts VIPs of the science world, as well as stars of big business seeking to spot talent and steal a few ideas. Dreams become reality here, or end up shattered.

It's showtime!

Behind the bewildering array of mad inventions is a smoothly organized, serious event. Contenders are given strictly controlled booth-space to set up their project and put across their idea. The judges then offer the best candidates a coveted spot at SFIT.

Live digital displays

DID YOU KNOW?

The showcase is a buzzing live show, where prospective students share technology that might just change the future.

Hydrodynamic engineering display

Lighting highlights entries

The Showcase Hall
One of the most exciting venues at SFIT is the Showcase Hall. Its imposing, traditional look hides the explosion of creative competition that goes on within.

Touchscreen display panels

Main walkway

Showcase presentation zone

Hiro's Microbots

When Hiro first unveils his microbot tech at the showcase, the crowd is unimpressed—it just looks like a tiny robot. Then something amazing happens. Thousands of microbots swarm together to build a tower, a huge hand, and even a giant pair of legs. Hiro's technology could change the world forever!

Micro servo-motors at all key nexus points

Master of microbots

Hiro wears a neural transmitter. This amazing piece of technology uses his thoughts to control the microbots. He simply has to think of what he wants them to do, and the microbots will do it!

Ball joints give maximum limb flexibility

ACTUAL SIZE

Powerful tool

A single microbot is small enough to grip between two fingers

Microbots can build in minutes something that would take months to build by hand. They can also lift and move almost any object with complete ease. They are an amazing tool, but in the wrong hands they could be a dangerous weapon.

KREI TECH INDUSTRIES

Microbots in micro-detail

Connectors telescope into microbot's body

Electro-magnetic connectors link microbots

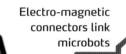

- Utilizes "swarm tech" hub mind
- Multi-mode morphing program
- Lightweight carbon fiber shell
- Mag-power connectors

A generous offer?

Alistair Krei, CEO of Krei Tech, is blown away by Hiro's work. The crowd is astonished when the billionaire businessman asks to buy the microbot technology, but Hiro refuses his offer.

> **"THE APPLICATIONS OF THIS TECH ARE LIMITLESS."**
>
> –HIRO

A friendly face

Hiro's personal hero, Professor Callaghan, is one of the judges at the showcase. Hiro is overjoyed when Callaghan offers him a place at SFIT.

Loss and Grief

What should have been the best day of Hiro's life turns into the worst. Just after he is offered a place at SFIT, a fire mysteriously breaks out at the Tech Showcase. Tadashi fearlessly runs back inside to rescue Professor Callaghan.

1 Fire at the showcase

Hiro asks Tadashi to stay, but his brave brother disappears into the burning building. Before Hiro can react, a massive explosion occurs. All that Hiro has left of his brother is Tadashi's favorite cap.

Cass opens Hiro's blinds to brighten up his room

Hiro stays in his room to avoid company

2 Tributes

A memorial is set up at the college to celebrate the lives of Callaghan and Tadashi, who were lost in the blaze. Students light candles and leave their own flower tributes.

3 A sad day

It is a suitably miserable day when the friends gather for Tadashi's funeral. Although they are all grieving, it makes everyone feel better when they share their loss together.

4 Hiro alone

Tadashi has always been there for Hiro, and now he can't imagine a future alone. Hiro sinks into a lonely depression and misses the start of college. He doesn't realize it, but life will soon get better.

Tadashi's things are left untouched

> **"WISH YOU WERE HERE, BUDDY."**
>
> –WASABI

5 Support group

Aunt Cass closes the café and invites everyone back home to share memories of Tadashi. Honey, Wasabi, Fred, and Go Go do their best to help Aunt Cass and Hiro with their sense of loss.

Baymax is Back!

Hiro sinks into a life of gloom after the loss of his brother, Tadashi. He hides away in his room, hardly eating, not even bothering to reply to letters from San Fransokyo Tech. But help is at hand, in an unexpected form...

1 Hopping mad

Just when Hiro thinks his life can't get any worse he experiences the brief—but intense—agony of stubbing his toe. He grabs his sore foot, hops around, and cries out in pain.

2 House call

Hearing an inflating sound, Hiro turns to see a friendly form rise up as if from nowhere. It is Baymax, the personal healthcare companion built by his brother! The sound of Hiro's pain has activated the bot.

Robotics books —untouched for weeks

3 On the case

In no mood to be fussed over, Hiro tries to get Baymax to switch himself off again right away. He tells the robot he is fine—but Baymax isn't so sure. He scans his new patient and finds lots to worry about!

4 Surprise diagnosis

Baymax states that he has detected high hormone levels in Hiro. The diagnosis is mood swings, common in adolescence. Hiro is unimpressed with the diagnosis, and tries to get Baymax back inside his case.

Baymax inflates at sound of pain

5 Crying face?

Baymax wants Hiro to describe the pain he is feeling, using Tadashi's emoticons. Despite Hiro's urging, he won't abandon a patient until they are satisfied with their care.

"ON A SCALE OF ONE TO TEN, HOW WOULD YOU RATE YOUR PAIN?"

-BAYMAX

Baymax's Vision

This ever-friendly healthcare companion is a unique creation, and he sees the world in his own way. His hyperspectral camera eyes relay complicated data back to his computer brain, which projects the information onto an internal screen for him to study and make his diagnosis.

Hyperspectral cameras
Lenses pick up data invisible to the human eye, such as body heat and oxygen saturation of the blood.

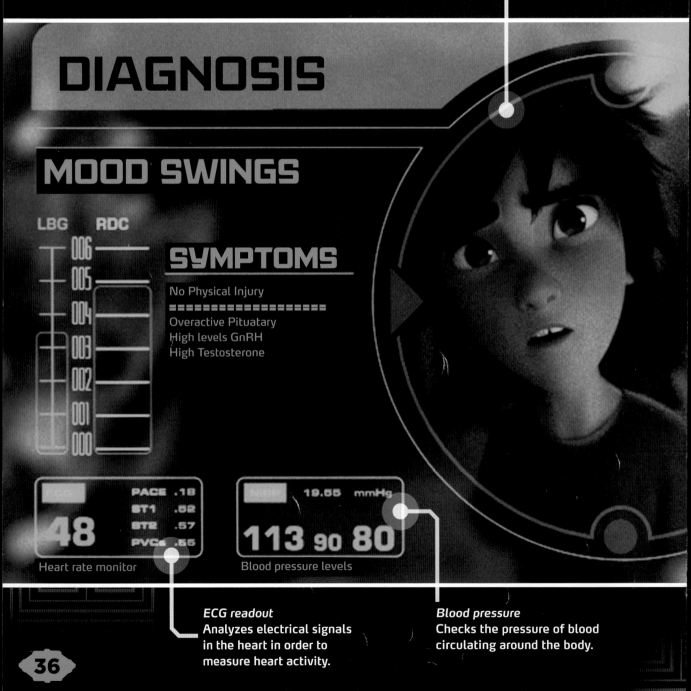

DIAGNOSIS

MOOD SWINGS

LBG RDC

006
005
004
003
002
001
000

SYMPTOMS

No Physical Injury
====================
Overactive Pituatary
High levels GnRH
High Testosterone

PACE .18
ST1 .52
ST2 .57
PVCs .55

48

Heart rate monitor

19.55 mmHg

113 90 80

Blood pressure levels

ECG readout
Analyzes electrical signals in the heart in order to measure heart activity.

Blood pressure
Checks the pressure of blood circulating around the body.

Patient feedback display

Clear, user-friendly explanations of his medical analysis are absolutely vital for Baymax's patients. His vinyl body acts as a screen to display his findings. Relevant areas are highlighted in simple diagrams using soothing colors to prevent patient anxiety.

Neurological mapping
Electrical impulses in the brain are monitored to check senses and motion centers.

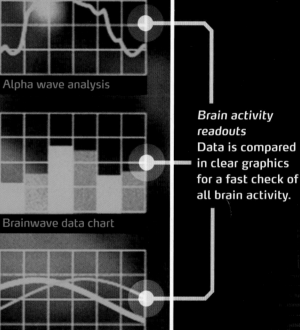

ADULT:

Typical adult brainwaves

Alpha wave analysis

SUBJECT:

Subject brainwaves

Brainwave data chart

Delta/theta comparison

Brain activity readouts
Data is compared in clear graphics for a fast check of all brain activity.

Continuous data log

79 34 70 65 60 47

Vital signs
Baymax can rapidly crunch numbers and work out Hiro's needs from complicated statistical analysis.

Microbot Attack!

After the fire at the Tech Showcase, Hiro never expects to see his microbots again—and he certainly doesn't expect to be attacked by an army of them! A shock find leads to a bizarre adventure with Baymax... who is really only trying to improve Hiro's health!

1 An unexpected discovery

Hiro trips over Baymax and falls onto his bedroom floor, where he notices something weird—the hoodie under his bed is vibrating. A microbot he left in its pocket wants to go somewhere...

"COME ON! LET'S GET OUT OF HERE! GO! HURRY!"

-HIRO

2 A robot about town

Hiro accidentally sends Baymax on a mission when he casually suggests he should find out where the microbot wants to go. Taking Hiro literally, Baymax obediently sets off across town with the microbot, as Hiro chases after him.

3 The warehouse

Baymax's quest takes him to an old, abandoned-looking warehouse. When Hiro catches up, he points out that the place is locked. Baymax, however, spots an open window—he has to deflate to squeeze through it!

4 Yokai!

When the determined pair get inside the warehouse, they discover a machine producing thousands of new microbots. This microbot army is under the control of a sinister masked figure. Under attack, Hiro and Baymax flee for their lives!

5 No help

The local police don't believe Hiro when he tells them that a man in a mask attacked him with an army of tiny robots! If Hiro wants to solve this mystery, he will have to do it on his own.

Yokai

This sinister super villain hides his identity behind a scary mask. Hiro realizes that Yokai must have started the fire at the Tech Showcase and stolen his microbots, but why? What is Yokai planning? And most importantly, who is he?

Mask detaches from skullcap

Bulky outfit disguises body shape

Sinister purpose

At the Tech Showcase, Hiro bragged that his microbots had limitless uses. Now that they've fallen into the hands of this mysterious enemy, who knows what dark schemes he will use them for? One thing is certain— Yokai will try to crush anyone who gets in his way!

Masked menace

Yokai wears a traditional Japanese Noh theater mask. The red markings on its face are meant to symbolize anger.

Carbon fiber gloves

The new master

A neural transmitter in Yokai's mask enables him to control Hiro's microbots, forming them into a nasty array of deadly weapons and cunning traps.

DID YOU KNOW?

Yōkai is an ancient Japanese word meaning "ghost," or "bad guy."

Prepare for Battle

It's a shock for Hiro to discover that someone has stolen his tech and is building a microbot army. It's even worse when he realizes that this enemy must have deliberately started the fire that killed Tadashi, in order to cover his tracks at the showcase. Hiro sets off on the dangerous path of revenge...

1 Upgrade time

Now that Hiro is determined to take on his sinister enemy, he needs serious back-up—it's time to upgrade Baymax. Hiro makes a new chip which gives Baymax some feisty karate moves. The gentle robot needs to toughen up, too, so Hiro builds him some mean armor.

2 Karate bot

It's time to try out Baymax's new fighting chip. Hiro has programmed the helpful bot to unleash the hammer fist, knife hand, side kick, and back kick. In his new, non-cuddly armor Baymax can easily punch through a wooden board!

New carbon fiber armor

Hiro's garage serves as a training ground

3 Return to the warehouse

Hiro thinks they are all set for a showdown with their foe. They return to the villain's hideaway, and Baymax kicks the door open... but the warehouse is now empty. Hiro's microbot is now indicating that it wants to head elsewhere. The unwavering pair follow the jumpy microbot, as they close in on their target.

> # "OKAY BAYMAX, TIME TO USE THOSE UPGRADES."
> –HIRO

Hiro takes cover before Baymax easily smashes the warehouse door down.

4 Down at the docks

The trail takes them down to the waterfront. Peering around a container they spot their enemy moving some strange equipment across the bay using the microbots. What is the masked menace up to? Before they can find out, Hiro's friends unexpectedly arrive. They were worried about Hiro, so they followed him, but their arrival means trouble...

Trouble at the Docks

Hiro leads his friends into trouble when he tries to solve the mystery of who is using his microbots. When he and Baymax track the enemy down to the docks, they are not expecting to be followed by Fred, Go Go, Wasabi, and Honey. Soon the whole gang is in serious danger...

1 Chased by Yokai

Realizing he is being spied on, Yokai launches an attack on the gang. Hiro wants to stay and fight, but after Yokai hurls a shipping container at them, his friends decide it's time to grab Hiro and get out of there. Yokai wants no witnesses and sets off in pursuit.

Baymax's added weight makes car hard to steer

Wasabi's small car is not an ideal getaway vehicle

Microbots can overcome any obstacle

2 Into the bay

Wasabi panics as Yokai catches up with the fleeing car. Go Go takes over driving, but Yokai creates a ramp of microbots beneath the vehicle forcing it upward, then turns the ramp into a tunnel, so no one can see where they're going. They think they are speeding to safety, but end up plunging into the bay!

3 No escape?

It looks like curtains for the gang as the car quickly starts to fill up with water, with them trapped inside! As it sinks to the bottom, Yokai watches, satisfied with his work.

4 Saved by Baymax

All is not lost... Baymax ditches his battered armor and reverts to his soft, huggable form. Inflating himself bigger than ever before, he rises upward, lifting all the friends to the surface with him. Everyone is elated to be alive, but ever-focused Baymax notes that they all have low temperatures and villain-related trauma.

"WHY ARE YOU TRYING TO KILL US?!"

-WASABI

Baymax 2.0

After their first battle against Yokai ends badly, Hiro realizes that Baymax will need a more serious upgrade. He gets some cool ideas from looking at Fred's collection of action figures. Soon Baymax 2.0 is the biggest action figure in town, but he still prefers healing people to fighting them.

To the max
Hiro's battle bot-building skills come in handy when it comes to making Baymax more awesome. All he has to do is scale up. A 3-D printer makes his new armor in no time!

TRUE OR FALSE?
Baymax's new thrusters are located in his legs.

TRUE: There isn't room for them anywhere else!

Upgraded hands can bend solid steel with ease

Power punch
On top of his karate skills, Baymax now has a spectacular new combat weapon—his rocket fists. Powered-up, they can blast off and smash holes in almost anything.

ベイマックス

Lean mean flying machine

Baymax is air-bound with newly added thrusters combined with fold-out wings. It would be great if he also knew how to steer, but luckily Hiro is there to give him instructions.

Super sensor visor

Bird-design wings with metal feather sections

New armor protects against blast or impact damage

SUPER ABILITIES

- Flight power
- Rocket fists
- Super sensor
- Martial arts

Rocket fist slots into forearm

Thrusters built into leg sections

"FUNCTIONALITY IMPROVED. 1000% INCREASE IN RANGE."

Super Hiro

Hiro knows he and his friends will need to become much stronger before they try to defeat Yokai. Building Baymax 2.0 was just the start—Hiro is going to use his robotics skills to upgrade the rest of the gang, too, starting with himself!

TRUE OR FALSE?

Hiro's suit has electro-magnets inside it.

TRUE: He uses them to attach to Baymax.

Electro-magnetic gauntlets have built-in kevlar armor protection

Gadget pouch

Flying fighters

When Baymax goes into flying mode, Hiro locks onto him with his magnetic pads and gloves. This means the two can fly as one.

Electro-magnetically soled boots

Heroic duo

Unlike the rest of the gang, Hiro doesn't fight by himself—he and Baymax fight alongside each other as a tightly knit unit. This takes a while for them to master, but soon Baymax and Hiro are an unstoppable team!

Headset comms link

SUPER ABILITIES

- Genius level intelligence
- Robot building skills
- Unique relationship with Baymax
- Multi-function super suit

Electro-magnetic knee pads

"WE'RE GONNA CHANGE THE WORLD."

Magnetic marvel

Baymax can fly at incredible speeds. Anything not securely attached to him would be torn off, so the magnets in Hiro's suit are super-powerful.

Super Go Go

A speed-freak before she even got a super suit, Go Go was born to be a super hero. After a few issues with balance at high velocity, she quickly masters her new gear and learns death-defying tricks. Fearless Go Go can't resist doing high-speed stunt jumps and roll-landings!

Gloves prevent friction burns

Speed wheels

Experiments with mag-lev (magnetic-levitation) technology have enabled Go Go to create frictionless wheels that are super-fast. The wheels also act as shields and throwing discs.

Jointed body-armor for crash protection

Detachable wheels held on by magnets

"STOP WHINING— WOMAN UP!"

Aerodynamic fin controls airflow

Super slick
Go Go's suit is the most streamlined of all the team's costumes. It is designed to reduce drag and cut through the air. The unusual helmet is modeled after those used in Olympic speed-cycling events.

SUPER ABILITIES
- Super speed and agility
- Throwing discs that return magnetically
- At full speed, Go Go's mass creates a massive impact

Fast and Fiesty
Go Go guides the team in key decisions. She's the first to tell Hiro that he won't be facing his enemy alone, and she is quick to keep Wasabi in line whenever he wavers. She also stands up to Hiro when his desire for revenge threatens to go too far.

TRUE OR FALSE?
Go Go's helmet is based on a fighter pilot's.

FALSE: It's based on a cyclist's!

51

Super Wasabi

Even though Wasabi is a powerful figure, he is still a bag of nerves when going into battle, and jumps at the occasional shadow. His deadly laser gloves mean he can defend himself from almost any attack, but he is frankly more worried about people messing with his stuff.

TRUE OR FALSE?

Wasabi wears a bandana to protect his head.

FALSE: He just wears it to look cool!

Armored shoulder plates

Laser gloves

The super-hot plasma produced by Wasabi's gloves can form many differently shaped blades. These can slice through any known material with total ease.

Japanese boots known as *Jika-tabi* provide grip

ワサビ

"WE'RE NOT SUPER HEROES— WE'RE NERDS."

Superheated plasma

Smart visor filters out laser glare

Awesome armor

With samurai-style plated armor, Wasabi's suit is designed to afford him maximum protection from his own laser weapons. He wears a headset to link up with the rest of the team and a bandana just to look cool.

Warrior or worrier?

Wasabi is used to people expecting him to be tough and has learned to put on a fake swagger. The slightest unexpected danger, however, can freak him out. He is very methodical and always likes to have a working plan.

SUPER ABILITIES

- Physics genius
- Can generate laser blades
- Steel-cutting power
- Super organizational skills

Super Honey

Always upbeat, Honey becomes an unstoppable positive force when she goes into hero mode. Her eye-zapping costume reflects the energy and creativity she brings to the team, and her crazy array of chem-capsules can be just as surprising to her teammates as they are to her foes.

Potent purse

The strap of Honey's purse is a string of empty chem-capsules. These are passed into a micro chemical factory inside the bag, where syringes inject chemical cocktails into them. They are then released for use.

Chem-capsule interface shows chemical levels

Addicted to danger

Honey seems to get a buzz from danger. Luckily her chemistry background makes her a whiz at mixing volatile substances to stunning effect. Among her chem-capsule weapons are a quick-freeze capsule, an instant net, and a tough plaster shield. She can also trap enemies in special sticky goo.

TRUE OR FALSE?

Honey doesn't like dangerous situations.

FALSE: She loves them!

ハニーレモン

Long hair left untied, even in battle

Advanced polyethylene shell

Light but lethal

Honey's costume is the least armored of all the team's suits, in order to keep her light on her feet and swift in attack. The sleeves and leggings provide skin protection from chemical spillage.

"THAT WAS AMAZING!"

Stylish wedges give added grip

Super Fred

Fred makes a natural super hero—he actually thinks being attacked by super villains is cool. He is now living his dream and can't help speaking in a corny monologue just like a real comic book character. Although a soft-hearted dude, Fred is in touch with his inner monster.

Flame effect arm fins

Inside the monster
Fred's suit conceals a sophisticated flame-thrower, mounted just below his chest. The suit's feet have built-in pogo-bounce tech.

The Beast
Fred loves Japanese monster movies, and the design of his costume is meant to terrify. With horns, fins, claws, and more, it may seem cumbersome, but Fred wears so-called Kaiju monster suits for fun. He is completely at home in one.

"IT'S FRED TIME!"

Eye lens gives night vision

SUPER ABILITIES

- Super-jump
- Breathing fire (of all kinds)
- Smokescreen
- Sign spinning

Flames hot enough to melt steel

TRUE OR FALSE?

Fred's suit allows him to jump to great heights.

TRUE: Fred loves to super-jump into battle!

Carbon fiber claws provide extra grip

Burning sensation

Fred has complete control over his flame-thrower, enabling him to pick the right heat for any situation. Supernova, fireball, and flame-grilled are just some of the options.

Warning lights indicate portal is activated

Krei's mistake

During the critical test mission into the portal, technicians report an irregularity in the field harmonics. Krei thinks it is within acceptable parameters, and goes ahead with the ill-fated mission anyway.

DID YOU KNOW?

The sparrow is a symbol of unexpected fortune in Japanese folklore, and a reward for kindness.

Maintenance ramp for portal

One-pilot flight pod

Akuma Island

Just offshore of San Fransokyo bay is a secret test facility belonging to Krei Tech. Here, billions of dollars have been poured into Alistair Krei's "Project Silent Sparrow." It aims to achieve a scientific dream: teleportation.

Project Silent Sparrow

The technology behind this incredible experiment is housed in a vast chamber hidden away from all but a privileged few. Twin portals are powered up to open a path into an unknown dimension. But the technology is untested, and disaster looms...

Teleport field generated by inner ring

Landing zone to catch pod exiting portal

Intrepid pilot

The brave figure in the flight pod is Krei's test pilot. Krei has told her loved ones that the portal technology is safe, but no one truly knows what will happen.

Go Team!

The gang may have the tech skills to turn themselves into super heroes, but now they must prove they really have what it takes to battle a bad guy. Thanks to Baymax's super sensor they have tracked their enemy, Yokai, down to the portal lab on Akuma Island. There's no turning back now.

Battle in the portal lab

The intrepid gang arrives to find that the lab on Akuma Island has been totally destroyed. Project Silent Sparrow went badly wrong, and the test pilot was lost inside the portal! Yokai ambushes Hiro and his friends, but the heroic team surprise their foe by fighting back with their new powers. Hiro manages to knock Yokai's mask off, but the villain gets away with the last pieces of the portal.

Laser blades deflect microbot attack

Friendly fire
Go Go zooms in to battle Yokai, but she skids on a patch of ice created by one of Honey's chem-capsules. These individuals will have to learn the art of teamwork!

Monster versus monster
Using his super-jump and fire breath, Fred aims to barbecue the bad guy. But heroics aren't as easy as they look in comic books!

Yokai's microbots obey his thoughts

Helmet contains comm-link to Baymax

Baymax prepares to fly at Yokai

The final battle

When Hiro knocks off Yokai's mask, he is shocked to discover his true identity—it is someone he never dreamed could turn to villainy. Worst of all, they discover his true plan. The gang must regroup, and then face Yokai in a final, climactic battle.

"We didn't set out to be super heroes. But sometimes life doesn't go the way you planned. The good thing is my brother wanted to help a lot of people. And that's what we're going to do. Who are we?...

Honey

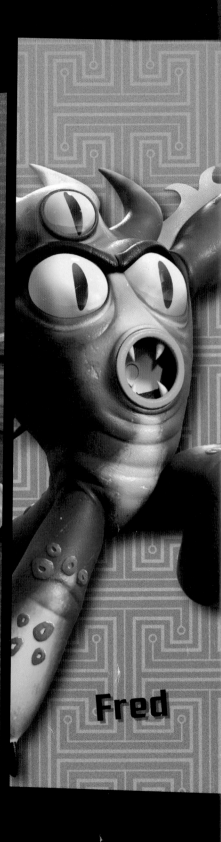

Fred

Wasabi

Acknowledgments

LONDON, NEW YORK,
MELBOURNE, MUNICH, AND DELHI

Editor David Fentiman
Senior Designer Lisa Robb
Design by Mark Richards, Lisa Robb, Toby Truphet
Pre-Production Producer Siu Yin Chan
Senior Producer Alex Bell
Managing Editor Laura Gilbert
Managing Art Editor Maxine Pedliham
Art Director Lisa Lanzarini
Publisher Julie Ferris
Publishing Director Simon Beecroft

First published in the United States
in 2014 by DK Publishing
345 Hudson Street, New York, New York 10014

10 9 8 7 6 5 4 3 2 1
001–255726–September/14

Page design copyright © 2014 Dorling Kindersley Limited

Published in Great Britain by Dorling Kindersley Limited
A Penguin Random House Company

A catalog record for this book is available
from the Library of Congress.

ISBN 978-1-4654-2270-5

Color reproduction by Altaimage, UK
Printed and bound in the USA by Lake Book Manufacturing, Inc.

DK would like to thank Danny Saeva, Heather Knowles,
Maria Elena Naggi, Winnie Ho, and Chelsea Alon at Disney Publishing,
Renato Lattanzi at Disney Consumer Products, and Roy Conli,
Lauren Brown, Albert Ramirez, and Andy Sinur at
Disney Animation Studios.